Stop that Train!

by Rachel Russ
Illustrated by Emma Levey

Pip and Kit get lost things back.

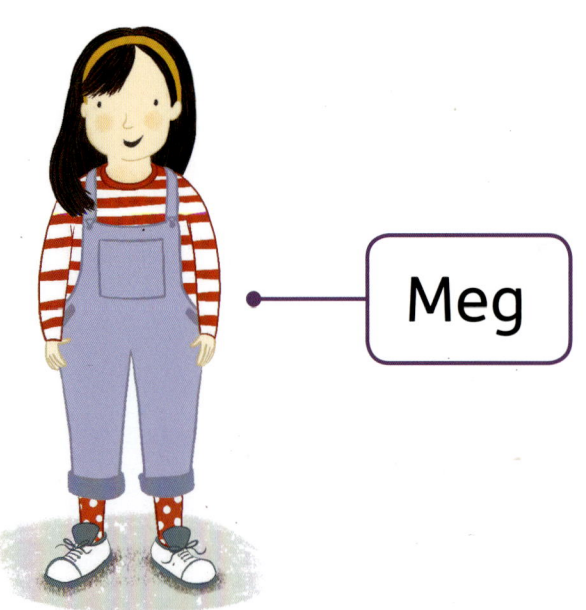

Pip and Kit get a text.
Meg has left her box on the train!

At the beginning of the story, Pip and Kit find out that Meg has left her box on the train. What do you think might happen next?

Pip and Kit set off along the road at high speed.

Pip and Kit must get to the train.

"I can see the train."

The train looks tiny because it is so far away.
Can you think of another word for 'tiny'?

The road bends to the right.

Pip and Kit are not <u>able</u> to catch up with the train. Why are they not <u>able</u> to catch up with it?

Pip and Kit jump on a sailing boat.

The boat cannot keep up with the train.

Pip and Kit get a lift in a van.

The van keeps up with the train.

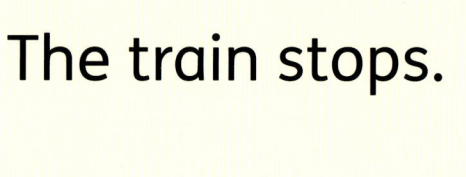

The train stops.

We need to go again!

Quick, Pip!

Pip and Kit are beside the train. What else can you see beside the train?

Pip and Kit get the box.

Meg has got her box back.

Pip and Kit are at the <u>entrance</u> to Meg's house.
Describe the <u>entrance</u>.

Retell the story